Army of Metalloids

At Our Doorstep

Deepak Singh

ISBN 978-93-5559-012-1
© Deepak Singh 2021
Published in India 2021 by Pencil

Contributors:
Editor: Deepak Singh

A brand of
One Point Six Technologies Pvt. Ltd.
123, Building J2, Shram Seva Premises,
Wadala Truck Terminal, Wadala (E)
Mumbai 400037, Maharashtra, INDIA
E connect@thepencilapp.com
W www.thepencilapp.com

Author biography

Army Of Metalloids Author Deepak Singh

Deepak Singh was born in the Indian city of Kharagpur in the year 1994. He was captivated by cricket, football, the universe, mankind, research, and technology as a child, and this fascination led to some early exposure to reading because he was drawn to stories about technology and study. Mr Deepak, who now works as a Research Analyst, developed an interest in concepts later on. Deepak examines the subject of how past events are irrevocable in "Army of Metalloids" by offering the capacity to modify previous events. Mr Deepak's debut novel is called Pi(π), Time and Nikola Tesla 369: Pi(π) Is Time. Lets Do Time Travel.

CONTENTS

Who are We

The only existing Homo species is We, modern humans. We haven't always been alone, though. All live humans are referred to be Homo sapiens, a species of highly intellectual primate. There were previously several species in the genus Homo, but all species and subspecies have become extinct save modern humans. The moniker Homo sapiens was first given to humans by Swedish scientist Carl Linnaeus in 1758. The name "homo sapiens" comes from Latin and means "intelligent man," according to the Encyclopedia Britannica.

What was the total number of early human species on the planet?

We used to not be alone as humans. There was a lot more human diversity a long time ago; roughly 300,000 years ago, Homo sapiens coexisted with an estimated eight now-extinct human species. We shared caverns with another human species called the Denisovans as recently as 15,000 years ago. And fossilised evidence suggests that there were many more early human species on the planet before our species arrived.

"Right now, we only have one human species," said Nick Longrich, an evolutionary scientist at the University of Bath in the United Kingdom. "We weren't all that special not long ago, but now we're the only ones left."

What was the total number of early human species?

When it comes to determining how many different species of humans existed, things become difficult fast, especially because researchers continue to uncover new fossils that turn out to be completely different and previously unknown species.

"The number is growing, and it depends on who you ask," said John Stewart, an evolutionary paleoecologist at Bournemouth University in the United Kingdom. According to some experts, Homo erectus is a composite of many species, including Homo georgicus and Homo ergaster. "It all comes down to how you define a species and how much variety you accept within it," Stewart told. "Because everyone wants an answer, it might turn into a rather unpleasant and pedantic debate. But, in reality, it is dependent."

What is the difference between a species and a group of species?

The concept of a species used to be straightforward: two individuals belonging to the same species could produce fruitful offspring. A horse and a donkey, for example, can mate to produce a mule, but mules are unable to reproduce. Horses and donkeys are not the same species, despite their biological resemblance. However, in recent decades, the simplicity of the definition of a species has given place to a more complicated scientific dispute. Some critics of the interbreeding concept argue that not all life reproduces sexually; for example, some plants and microbes can reproduce asexually. Others have proposed that we should put animals with comparable anatomical traits together to determine species, although this method has flaws as well. It's a very subjective approach to defining life because there can be significant morphological diversity between sexes and even individuals of the same species in various locations of the planet.

Biologists prefer to distinguish between species using DNA, and with advances in technology, they can do it with greater precision. However, we don't have the DNA of every ancient human - the Homo Erectus genome, for example, has never been sequenced. When you consider that up to 2% of the DNA of the typical European originates from Neanderthals, and up to 6% of the DNA of some Melanesians (Indigenous people from the islands just northeast of Australia in Oceania) comes from Denisovans, things get much murkier. So, are we a distinct species from our forefathers?

"Many people will tell you that Neanderthals and humans are the same species," Stewart explained. "They're merely a slightly different form of modern human, as evidenced by interbreeding, but the definition of species has moved on from interbreeding as well." After considering all of this, some scientists have concluded that the concept of a species does not exist. Others, however, argue that, while a precise definition of a species is very difficult to establish, it is nevertheless worthwhile to make the attempt so that we may talk about evolution — including our own species' evolution — in a sensible way.

We fumble on, knowing that a species might mean various things to different people, which means that opinions on the number of human species that have ever existed will differ. It's also a matter of defining what it means to be human. To answer this question, you must first comprehend the term hominin, which refers to a big group that includes humans and chimps who have a common ancestor.

"The chimpanzee and we share a common ancestor," Stewart explained. It's likely to be a diverse bunch if we conclude that humans are everything that arrived after our separation from ancient chimps some 6 million to 7 million years ago. Most scientists acknowledge at least 21 human species, according to the Smithsonian National Museum of Natural History. Granted, it's not an exhaustive list; the Denisovans, for example, are absent.

Homo sapiens, Neanderthals, Indonesian hobbits, Homo erectus, and Homo Naledi are among the species on the list. Other animals that lived closer to the common ancestor of humans and chimps, and hence resemble chimps more than modern humans, are also included on the list. These species are still referred to as early humans, despite their appearance. "You can't expect them to look like us 5 million years ago," Stewart explained.

According to Stewart, If the Smithsonian claims that there are twenty-one, you can bet the diversity is far higher. Because the list errs on the side of caution, it only includes species that are almost widely recognised. The Smithsonian's list, for example, does not include the recently discovered tiny human species Homo luzonensis, which is known only from a few bones found in a cave in the Philippines.

Researchers also believe that many more petrified species have yet to be discovered. "The list has just gotten longer and longer, and I don't see why that will change," Stewart added.

What makes you think that not all primates have evolved into humans?

Chimpanzees, our closest living relatives, stayed in the trees, eating fruit and hunting monkeys, while humans were travelling around the world, developing agriculture, and visiting the moon.

Contemporary chimps have been around for more than a million years longer than modern humans compared to 300,000 years for Homo sapiens, according to the latest estimates, yet we've been on divergent evolutionary pathways for 6 million or 7 million years. If we consider chimps to be our cousins, our last common ancestor is the equivalent of a great-great-grandmother with only two live descendants.

But why did one of her evolutionary children do so much more than the other?

"The reason other primates aren't turning into humans is that they're fine," Briana Pobiner, a paleoanthropologist at the Smithsonian Institute in Washington, D.C., explains. Mountain gorillas in Uganda, howler monkeys in the Americas and lemurs in Madagascar have all demonstrated that they can flourish in their natural environments.

"Evolution isn't a linear process" anthropology professor Lynne Isbell of the University of California, Davis, explained. "It's all about how well creatures fit into their existing habitats," says the researcher. Humans aren't "more evolved" than other primates, according to evolutionary biologists, and we surely haven't won the "evolutionary game." While humans' extraordinary flexibility allows us to manage a wide range of situations to satisfy our requirements, it isn't enough to propel us to the top of the evolutionary ladder.

Scientists believe that as ancestral humans began spending more time on the ground, they began to differentiate themselves from ancestral chimps. Isbell speculated that our forefathers were looking for food as they explored new habitats.

"The first noticeable behavioural change would have certainly been some difference in habitat choices," Isbell added. "Our forefathers would have ventured into ecosystems without closed canopies in order to begin bipedalism. In regions with more spread-out trees, they would have had to move more on the ground."

The rest is the narrative of human evolution. The chimps, on the other hand, did not stop evolving just because they stayed in the trees. Their ancestors parted from ancestral bonobos 930,000 years ago, according to genomic research published in 2010, while the founders of three surviving subspecies diverged 460,000 years ago. Only 93,000 years ago, central and eastern chimps diverged.

Evolution Of Modern Human Beings

An ancestral species of humans, chimps, and bonobos lived on the African continent about 6 million years ago. Around that time, one group of those ancient apes began to separate from the rest and became known as the hominins.

According to the Australian Museum, this hominin branch of the evolutionary tree contains current humans, extinct human species, and all of our direct relatives, including members of the genus Homo, Australopithecus, Paranthropus, and Ardipithecus. "Erect posture, bipedal movement, larger brains, and behavioural features such as specialised tool use and, in certain cases, communication through language have separated hominins from other primates, alive and extinct," noted Pontzer. Importantly, these qualities are a mix of physical and behavioural characteristics, which are the two main ways in which scientists distinguish H. sapiens from other species.

It took a few million years after hominins diverged from the other great apes for any Homo species to arise. "The initial populations of the Homo lineage evolved in Africa between approximately 3 and 2 million years ago from an unknown parent species," says the study.

The origins of the Homo genus are unknown. The earliest Homo fossil discovered to date, published in the journal Science in 2015, dates from around 2.8 million years ago, though scientists are unsure of which species it belongs to. The next-oldest fossil, discovered in a 2015 study published in the journal Nature, belonged to a person who lived roughly 2.3 million years ago and could have been Homo habilis. Stone tools were found with that fossil, indicating that the person who buried it knew how to utilise them.

Which Homo Species Are There?

According to human evolution expert Chris Stringer of the British Natural History Museum, the number of known Homo species has more than doubled in the previous 15 years, from four to nine. H. neanderthalensis (Neanderthals) and Homo erectus (ancient species) are now included in the genus (whose name translates to "upright man"). In a report, scientists described the most recent addition, H. luzonensis.

"There's a 195,000-year-old H. sapiens fossil from Ethiopia that exhibits the core traits of contemporary humans," Stringer told Live Science. "We found fossils that we can reasonably name H. sapiens from 195,000 years onwards."

However, there may be an even older case of H. sapiens: Fossilized remains discovered alongside stone tools in a Moroccan cave show that "modern" humans appeared as early as 315,000 years ago, according to a report in 2017.

Because there is no visible distinction between humans and our close cousins, scientists must rely on either anatomy or behaviour to distinguish human remains from others. Anatomists claim that the skeletons of H. sapiens can be used to identify them, whereas archaeologists argue that behaviour is what identifies modern humans.

A Human's Anatomical Definition

According to a 2015 assessment published in Science, scientists cannot agree on an exact definition of what characterises the species Homo. According to a review published in the Journal of Quaternary Science in 2019, most Homo species have "a long, low braincase and strong continuous brow ridge." Human beings, on the other hand, has distinct "modern" physical traits, such as a big rounded braincase, lack of a brow-ridge, a chin (even in infancy), and a narrow pelvis as compared to other Homo genus members.

However, Stringer believes that early human beings did not have all of the same characteristics as modern human beings. "Humans want to categorise and keep things easy," he explained, "but nature doesn't recognise our classifications."

A Human's Archaeological Definition

Some researchers believe that behaviour distinguishes H. sapiens from other Homo species, as well as all other creatures on the planet.

A wide range of behaviours can be classified as "human." Researchers enumerated features that have historically been used to identify human beings in a 2003 review published in the journal Current Anthropology. These featured, among other things, evidence of dead burials, ceremonial art, ornaments, crafted bone and antler material, blade technology, and fishing. The authors of that review did point out, however, that many of those practices are Eurocentric and may not apply to people in other regions of the world.

"What to call a contemporary person has been a long argument, and the debate is still going on," Bentsen added. Archaeologists are looking at what certain features say about cognition rather than a checklist of traits. Seasons or animal migrations, for example, are shown in engravings or symbols, implying that early humans were intelligent enough to comprehend those notions. "It demonstrates advanced intellect and planning," Bentsen said. "It's a sophisticated behaviour package," says the narrator.

However, evidence that other Homo species, such as Neanderthals, had similar capacities complicates the behavioural approach of differentiating modern humans. These stocky cave dwellers developed tools, buried their dead, and managed fire, all of which were long considered uniquely human actions. Stringer, in fact, discounts behaviour as a means of distinguishing species. He stated, "Behavior is not an acceptable way of designating a species." "It's a lot easier to share behaviour than it is to share anatomy."

Are Human Beings A Separate Species?

According to Encyclopedia Britannica, a species is defined as "groups of interbreeding natural populations that are reproductively isolated from other such groups." That concept, however, may not apply to Homo species, as evidence of interbreeding between Neanderthals, Homo sapiens, and Homo Denisovans have just been uncovered (a hominin species discovered in Denisova Cave in Russia). For example, evidence of many occurrences of interbreeding between Neanderthals and H.

sapiens was described in a 2018 research published in the journal Nature. Another Nature research published in 2018 provided evidence of an ancient human hybrid with Neanderthal and Denisovan ancestry.

According to Stringer, this has led some scientists to believe that numerous Homo species, including ours, should be grouped together. Modern people are Homo sapiens, Neanderthals are Homo sapiens neanderthalensis, and Denisovans are Homo sapiens Denisovans, according to this paradigm.

Stringer, on the other hand, believes that humans and Neanderthals are two distinct species with different bone structures. "If Neanderthals and Homo sapiens remained separate long enough to have such diverse skull forms, pelvises, and ear bones, they can be regarded as different species, interbreeding or not," he stated in a Natural History Museum paper.

What is Metalloid

A Metalloid is a substance that partially conducts current. Its conductivity is somewhere between that of a conductor with full conductivity and that of an insulator with negligible conductivity.

Your computer or smartphone, on which you are currently reading this, is actually powered by a bed of silicon covered with billions of transistors that are thinner than a strand of hair and are made of a solid substance known as a Metalloid.

What exactly is Metalloid? The movement of electricity and energy band.

Any crystal is made up of atoms with a high number of closely spaced energy levels in which electrons can be accommodated. Only two electrons spinning in opposite directions can house a single energy level, according to Pauli's exclusion principle, which is beyond the scope.

Certain levels are illustrated by lines separated by tiny distances where electrons are allowed to exist solely in these levels. After that, a few energy levels are combined together to form 'bands,' or energy bands. The valence band, which has the least amount of energy, is below it, while the conduction band, which has a higher level of energy, is above it. The bandgap energy is the amount of energy necessary for an electron to 'jump' this distance.

The crystal has an odd number of electrons in its valence band and none in the next, resulting in a solitary, loose electron at the highest energy level. When given a tiny kick or linked to a battery, this quickly flows to the conduction band, generating a large current. Conductors include metals such as copper and iron, and this crystal is one among them.

The second crystal's electrons are not only exceedingly stable and connected to each other, but there are also two electrons in its conduction band, making electron movement to the conduction band practically difficult. This is a representation of an insulator. Insulators such as paper, rubber, and glass are widespread.

A loose electron exists in the third crystal, but there is no vacant conduction band. It does, however, have half-filled energy levels that can hold more electrons. When given a strong enough kick, this loose electron can be propelled into the conduction band, resulting in a modest amount of current. Silicon and Germanium are two major examples of Metalloid.

A drawbridge analogy can be used to describe this operation, where the bridges representing conductors either overlap or unite to let people easily traverse.

Metalloid can be compared to a shoddy bridge that only closes halfway, requiring a traveller to leap the distance between them. Finally, an insulator is a bridge that never closes, making it impossible for any passenger to jump to the other side.

What distinguishes a Metalloid from other materials?

The movement of positive charges causes conductivity. Conductivity refers to a substance's ability to allow electrons to flow through it. Conductivity is highest in conductors and lowest in insulators because electrons move through them in a minimal amount. A Metalloid's conductivity, on the other hand, is moderate, as the name implies. Another fascinating feature of a Metalloid is that the current is carried not only by electrons but also by the holes that they leave behind. The holes in the valence band can be occupied by electrons from lower states, which contribute to current flow, leaving a hole in these deeper states as well, which will be occupied by electrons beneath, and so on.

As a result, the current can be defined as the rate at which these 'positive' charges flow.

Doping and current control through a device To comprehend its utility, one must first understand that, unlike a conductor, the current passing through a Metalloid is a delicate combination of charges and their continuous flow, rather than an unregulated surge of electrons. The idea of intentionally contaminating a silicon or germanium atom to induce new energy levels was proposed by innovative engineering.

Pure silicon atoms on the left. Silicon with Phosphorus doped in the centre, resulting in an extra electron. Right: Silicon with Boron doped in it, resulting in an extra hole.

Crystals with more valence electrons than a Metalloid (typically phosphorus), which tend to roam freely in the structure and contribute to the flow of electricity, or crystals with fewer electrons (aluminium), which borrow electrons from silicon and leave excess holes, contaminate materials. The contaminated silicon produced by phosphorus sprinkling is known as a 'n' type Metalloid, while the silicon produced by the latter procedure is known as a 'p' type Metalloid. The degree of contamination or doping determines how current is controlled.

The transistor was a watershed moment in electronic history.

Engineers used Metalloid' unique features to create small devices that control current flow in a circuit. Since its development in 1947, this gadget, known as a transistor, has altered the path of human history.

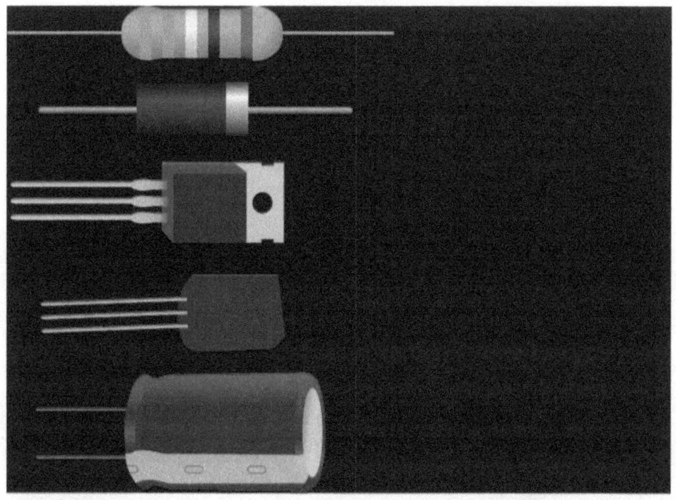

The disturbance that causes electrons to bounce and leap can also be caused by heating Metalloid to extremely high temperatures. As a result, these materials can act as conductors at high temperatures while also acting as insulators at lower temperatures (less jiggling). In wireless communication technology, transistors are commonly utilised as switching and amplification devices. Transistors of various sorts are seen on the left. Right: An n-p-n Bipolar Junction Transistor circuit; the base voltage or p-type Metalloid controls the amount of current flowing from the emitter to the collector.

Sandwiching a p-type material between two n-type materials or an n-type material between two p-type materials creates a transistor.

The voltage supplied to the p-type material controls and guides the current that flows from the heavily doped n-type material on one side to the relatively less doped n-type material on the other side, much like the knob on top of a tap. The current that is allowed to flow is denoted by a logic '1', while no current is denoted by a logic '0,' transforming them to binary digits, the computer's language. The transistors switch between these ones and zeroes, feeding a sequence of outputs – again, ones and zeroes – to another circuit as an input made up of similar transistors. Electron transfer from a high-doped zone to a low-doped region on the left. Right: A transistor serves as a pipe's tap, producing zero and one, respectively.

These switches are the building blocks of logic gates, which are the building blocks of a microprocessor, your computer's brain, and now our phones as well. According to Moore's Law, advanced technologies have aided in the reduction and scaling down of transistor sizes to nanometers, allowing a billion of them to be squeezed onto a tiny silicon chip. Their main issue isn't claustrophobia.

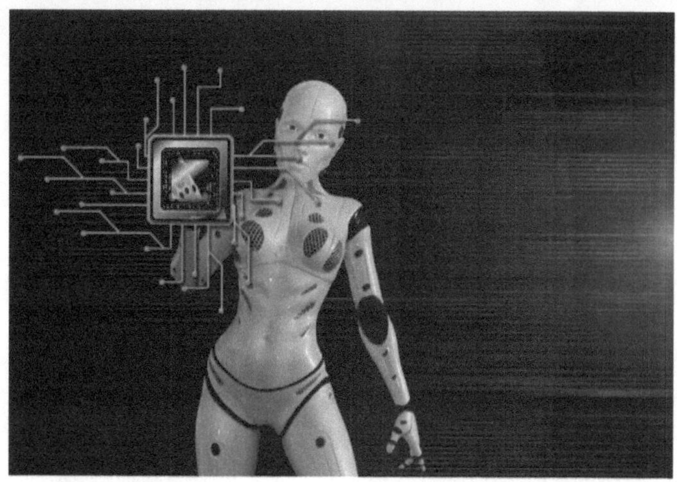

This is a significant advantage, and these materials have unquestionably altered the technological world. The transistor is without a doubt one of the most important innovations of the twentieth century, as Metalloid technologies have shaped and are moulded by the modern world. This is especially true when it comes to combining radio, television, e-mail, and dozens of other technologies into a single five-inch cuboid and linking people all over the world!

What is Artificial Intelligence Technology

Artificial intelligence (AI) is a broad field of computer science that focuses on creating intelligent machines that can accomplish activities that would normally need human intelligence. Although AI is a multidisciplinary discipline with many techniques, advances in machine learning and deep learning are causing a paradigm shift in almost every industry.

Alan Turing changed history for the second time with a simple question: "Can machines think?" Less than a decade after unlocking the Nazi encryption machine Enigma and helping the Allies win World War II, mathematician Alan Turing changed history once more with a simple question: "Can computers think?"

The core purpose and vision of artificial intelligence were set by Turing's paper "Computing Machinery and Intelligence" (1950) and the Turing Test that followed.

At its most basic level, AI is a discipline of computer science whose goal is to answer yes to Turing's question. It is the goal of artificial intelligence researchers to reproduce or duplicate human intellect in robots.

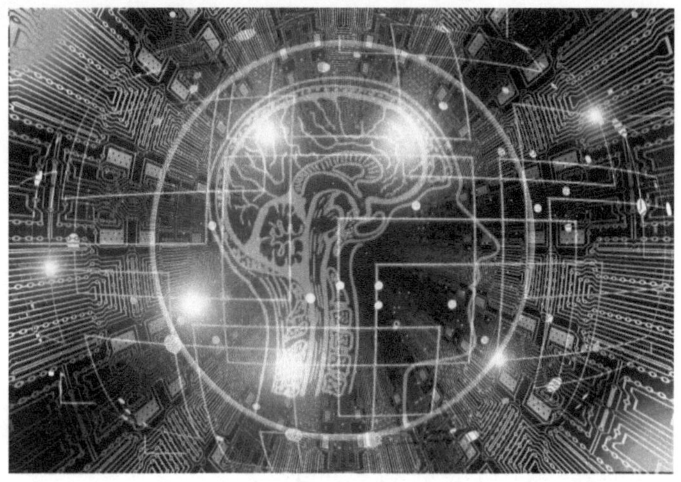

Artificial intelligence's broad purpose has sparked a slew of questions and arguments. So much so that there is no commonly acknowledged definition of the field.

The biggest flaw in just defining AI as "creating intelligent machines" is that it fails to describe what artificial intelligence is. What distinguishes a machine as intelligent?

Stuart Russell and Peter Norvig addressed the subject in their pioneering textbook Artificial Intelligence: A Modern Approach by uniting their work around the idea of intelligent agents in machines. AI is defined as "the study of agents that receive percepts from the environment and perform actions," according to this definition. (viii) Russell and Norvig.

Norvig and Russell then go on to look at four main approaches to AI that have shaped the discipline in the past:

Human-like thinking

Reasonable thinking

Humane behaviour

Rational decision-making

The first two concepts are about thinking and cognitive processes, whereas the rest are about conduct. "All the capabilities needed for the Turing Test also allow an agent to operate rationally," Norvig and Russell write, focusing on rational agents that behave to get the best outcome. (Russel and Norvig 4, for example.)

"Algorithms enabled by limitations, exposed by representations that support models focused at loops that tie thought, perception, and action together," says Patrick Winston, the Ford professor of artificial intelligence and computer science at MIT.

While these concepts may appear esoteric to the common person, they assist to focus the discipline as a branch of computer science and provide a roadmap for incorporating machine learning and other artificial intelligence subsets into machines and programmes.

Jeremy Achin, CEO of DataRobot, opened his keynote at the Japan AI Experience in 2017 by giving the following characterization of how AI is used today:

"Artificial intelligence (AI) is a computer system that can do tasks that would normally need human intelligence... Many of these artificial intelligence systems are based on machine learning, while others are based on deep learning and yet others are based on mundane things like rules."

How Does Artificial Intelligence Work?

Artificial intelligence can be divided into two categories:

Narrow AI, often known as "Weak AI," is a type of artificial intelligence that functions in a constrained setting and simulates human intellect. While narrow AI is frequently focused on executing a specific task very well, these machines operate under many more constraints and limits than even the most basic human intelligence.

Artificial General Intelligence (AGI): AGI, often known as "Strong AI," is the type of artificial intelligence that we see in movies like Westworld's machines or Star Trek: The Next Generation's Data. AGI is a machine that has general intelligence and can use that intelligence to solve any problem, much as a person can.

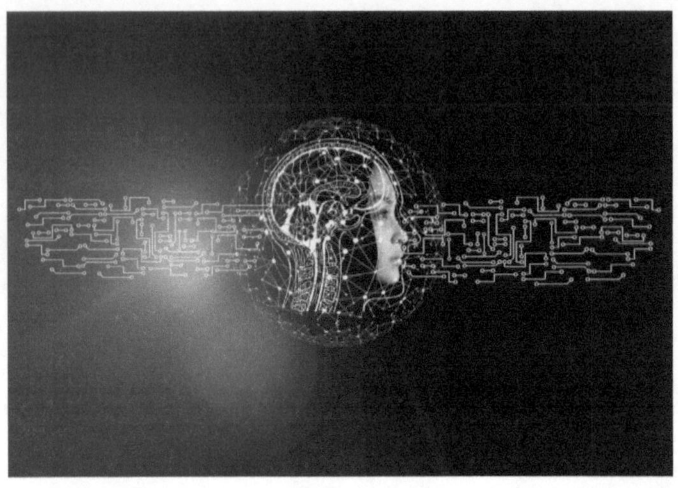

EXAMPLES OF ARTIFICIAL INTELLIGENCE

1. Intelligent assistants (like Siri and Alexa)

2. Tools for disease mapping and prediction

3. Drone robots and manufacturing

4. Recommendations for tailored healthcare therapy that are optimised

5. Bots that converse with customers for marketing and customer service

6. Stock trading Robo-advisors

7. Email spam filters

8. Tools for monitoring social media for potentially harmful content or fake information

Artificial Intelligence with a Limited Scope

Narrow AI is all around us, and it is by far the most successful implementation of AI too far. Narrow AI has made major advancements in the recent decade as a result of its emphasis on executing certain tasks, which have resulted in "substantial societal advantages and have contributed to the nation's economic vitality. According to the Obama Administration's 2016 report "Preparing for the Future of Artificial Intelligence."

Here are a few instances of Narrow AI:

1. Image recognition software can be found by searching on Google.

2. Personal assistants such as Siri, Alexa, and others.

3. Automobiles that drive themselves.

4. Watson is an IBM product.

Deep Learning & Machine Learning

Machine learning and deep learning advancements are at the heart of Narrow AI. It might be difficult to tell the difference between artificial intelligence, machine learning, and deep learning. Frank Chen, a venture capitalist, gives a fair explanation of how to tell them apart, noting:

"Artificial intelligence is a collection of algorithms and intelligence designed to imitate human intellect. One of these is machine learning, and deep learning is one of the machine learning approaches."

Simply defined, machine learning feeds data to a computer and employs statistical techniques to help it "learn" how to be better at a task without being particularly programmed for it, reducing the need for millions of lines of written code. Unsupervised learning (using labelled data sets) and supervised learning (using unlabeled data sets) are both types of machine learning (using unlabeled data sets).

Deep learning is a sort of machine learning that processes data through a neural network design inspired by biology. The data is processed through a number of hidden layers in the neural networks, which allows the machine to go "deep" in its learning, creating connections and weighing input for the best outcomes.

General Artificial Intelligence (AGI)

For many AI researchers, the creation of a machine with human-level intellect that can be applied to any activity is the Holy Grail, yet the road to AGI has proven difficult.

The hunt for a "universal algorithm for learning and acting in any environment" (Russel and Norvig 27) isn't new, but the difficulties of constructing a machine with a complete set of cognitive abilities haven't become any easier.

AGI has long been the subject of dystopian science fiction, in which super-intelligent robots take over humans, but scientists believe that it isn't something we should be concerned about anytime soon.

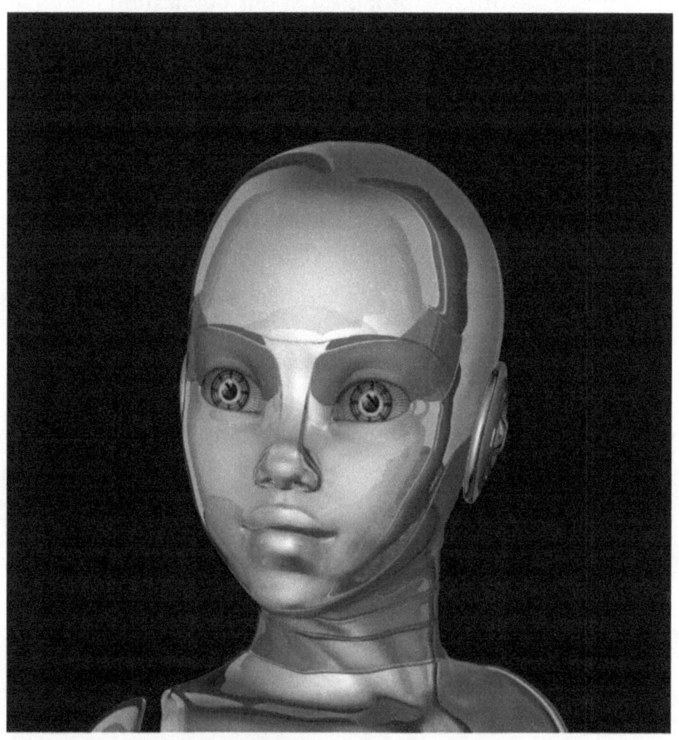

History Of Artificial Intelligence

Ancient Greek mythology included intelligent robots and artificial entities for the first time. The creation of syllogism and its application of deductive reasoning by Aristotle was a watershed point in humanity's search to comprehend its own intelligence.

1. The year was 1943. "A Logical Calculus of Ideas Immanent in Nervous Activity," by Warren McCullough and Walter Pitts, is published. The first mathematical model for developing a neural network was proposed in this publication.

2. In the year 1949, Donald Hebb advances the hypothesis that brain pathways are formed by experiences and that connections between neurons become stronger the more they are used in his book The Organization of Behavior: A Neuropsychological Theory. In AI, Hebbian learning remains an essential model.

3. Alan Turing publishes "Computing Machinery and Intelligence" in 1950, suggesting the Turing Test, a method for detecting whether or not a machine is intelligent.

4. SNARC, the first neural network computer, was built by Harvard undergraduates Marvin Minsky and Dean Edmonds.

5. The paper "Programming a Computer for Playing Chess" by Claude Shannon is published.

6. The "Three Laws of Robotics" are published by Isaac Asimov.

7. The year 1952, Arthur Samuel creates a checkers self-learning programme.

8. In the year 1954, In the Georgetown-IBM machine translation experiment, 60 carefully

selected Russian sentences are mechanically translated into English.

9. In the year 1956, At the "Dartmouth Summer Research Project on Artificial Intelligence," the term "artificial intelligence" was developed. The conference, which established the scope and goals of AI and was led by John McCarthy, is largely regarded as the genesis of artificial intelligence as we know it today.

10. The first thinking programme, Logic Theorist (LT), is demonstrated by Allen Newell and Herbert Simon.

11. The year 1958, The AI programming language Lisp is created by John McCarthy, who also publishes the paper "Programs with Common Sense." The paper proposed the Advice Taker, a complete AI system capable of learning from experience in the same way as humans do.

12. In the year 1959, The General Problem Solver (GPS) is a programme created by Allen Newell, Herbert Simon, and J.C. Shaw to mimic human problem-solving.

13. The Geometry Theorem Prover programme was created by Herbert Gelernter.

14. While working at IBM, Arthur Samuel coined the term "machine learning."

15. The MIT Artificial Intelligence Project was founded by John McCarthy and Marvin Minsky.

16. In the year 1963, Stanford's AI Lab is founded by John McCarthy.

17. The year 1966, The US government's Automatic Language Processing Advisory Committee (ALPAC) report exposes the lack of progress in machine translation research, a key Cold War programme that promised automatic and instantaneous Russian translation. All government-funded MT projects have been cancelled as a result of the ALPAC study.

18. The year was 1969. DENDRAL, a XX programme, and MYCIN, a blood infection diagnostic system, are the first successful expert systems established at Stanford.

19. The year 1972, PROLOG, a logic programming language, is created.

20. The year was 1973. The British government releases the "Lighthill Report," which details the failures of AI research and leads to significant cuts in funding for AI initiatives.

21. From 1974 till 1980, Frustration with AI development leads to significant DARPA cuts in research grants. Artificial intelligence funding is drying up, and research is stalling, according to the ALPAC study and the previous year's "Lighthill Report." The "First AI Winter" is the name given to this period.

22. R1 (also known as XCON) is the first successful commercial expert system, developed by Digital Equipment Corporations in 1980. R1, which is designed to configure orders for new computer systems, kicks off a decade-long investment boom in expert systems, essentially ending the first "AI Winter."

23. The year was 1982. The ambitious Fifth Generation Computer Systems project is launched by Japan's Ministry of International Trade and Industry. The purpose of FGCS is to create a platform for AI development and supercomputer-like performance.

24. The year was 1983. In reaction to Japan's FGCS, the US government announces the Strategic Computing Initiative, which will support advanced computing and artificial intelligence research through DARPA.

25. In the year 1985, Expert systems cost more than a billion dollars each year, and an entire business called the Lisp machine market has sprung up to support them. Symbolics and Lisp Machines Inc., for example, create specialised computers that run the AI programming language Lisp.

26. From 1987 to 1993, The Lisp machine industry failed 1987, ushering in the "Second AI Winter," as computing technology advanced and cheaper competitors appeared. Expert systems became too expensive to operate and update during this time, and they finally fell out of favour.

27. In 1992, Japan stops the FGCS project due to a failure to reach the ambitious targets set out a decade before.

28. After spending nearly $1 billion and falling far short of predictions, DARPA ended the Strategic Computing Initiative in 1993.

29. During the Gulf War in 1991, US forces used DART, an automated logistical planning and scheduling programme.

30. Deep Blue, an IBM computer, defeated world chess champion, Gary Kasparov, in 1997.

31. The self-driving automobile STANLEY wins the DARPA Grand Challenge in 2005.

32. The US military is beginning to invest in self-driving robots such as Boston Dynamic's "Big Dog" and iRobot's "PackBot."

33. Google achieves improvements in speech recognition in 2008, and the functionality is made available via its iPhone app.

34. On Jeopardy! in 2011, IBM's Watson beats the competition!

35. The year 2012, Andrew Ng, the Google Brain Deep Learning project's founder, feeds 10 million YouTube videos into a neural network using deep learning algorithms as a training set. The neural network learns to recognise a cat without being

informed what a cat is, ushering in a new era of deep learning funding and neural networks.

36. In 2014, Google's self-driving car becomes the first to pass a state driving exam.

37. World champion Go player Lee Sedol is defeated by Google DeepMind's AlphaGo in 2016. The ancient Chinese game's complexity was seen as a significant barrier to overcome in AI.

Robotic Process Automation

Robotic process automation is a term that refers to the automation of robotic processes. RPA is a type of technology that automates business processes by using business logic and organised inputs. An organisation may use RPA tools to set up the software, or a "robot," to capture and interpret applications for things like processing transactions, manipulating data, triggering responses, and interacting with other digital systems. RPA scenarios can be as easy as sending an automated email response to as complex as deploying thousands of bots to automate jobs in an ERP system.

According to Regina Viadro, vice president of EPAM Systems and adviser of the company's IA practise, financial services COOs is at the forefront of RPA adoption, finding out ways to use software to accelerate business processes without increasing headcount or costs. Viadro has completed RPA engagements with clients in financial services, healthcare, retail, and human resources, demonstrating the wide range of RPA applications available today.

What are the advantages of robotic process automation (RPA)?

RPA allows businesses to save money on staffing and eliminate human error. A bank's experience with RPA, according to David Schatsky, a managing director at Deloitte LLP, was that the bank redesigned its claims process by deploying 85 bots to operate 13 systems, handling 1.5 million requests per year. According to Schatsky, the bank added capacity equal to more than 200 full-time workers for around a third of the cost of hiring more people.

Bots are usually low-cost and simple to set up, since they don't require any custom software or extensive system integration. Such characteristics, according to Schatsky, are critical as businesses seek to expand without incurring significant costs or causing tension among employees. "By automating low-value activities, companies are trying to get some breathing room so they can better serve their business," Schatsky says.

Companies can also boost their automation efforts by combining RPA with cognitive technology like machine learning, speech recognition, and natural language processing to automate higher-order tasks that previously involved human perception and judgement.

According to Viadro, RPA implementations that include 15 to 20 steps are part of a value chain known as intelligent automation (IA). "If we segmented all of the big companies and asked them what's on their agenda for 2018, almost all will say intelligent automation," says Viadro.

According to Gartner, automation and artificial intelligence would minimise employee requirements in company shared-service centres by 65 per cent by 2020. The RPA market is expected to reach $1 billion by 2020. At that time, 40% of large businesses would have implemented RPA software, compared to less than 10% today.

See "Why bots are poised to disrupt the enterprise" and "Robotic process automation is a killer app for cognitive computing" for more information on RPA's benefits.

What are RPA's drawbacks?

RPA isn't right for every business. RPA, like any other automation technology, has the ability to reduce jobs, posing a challenge for CIOs in terms of talent management. Although RPA-enabled businesses are attempting to move many employees to new roles, Forrester Research estimates that RPA software could endanger the employment of 230 million or more information workers, or about 9% of the global workforce.

RPA implementations fail more often than not, even though CIOs navigate the human capital conundrum. In a May 2017 paper, McKinsey & Company senior partners Alex Edlich and Vik Sohoni said, "Several robotics programmes have been placed on hold, or CIOs have flatly declined to instal new bots."

According to Edlich and Sohoni, installing thousands of bots has taken much longer and is much more complicated and expensive than most organisations had anticipated.

The platforms on which bots communicate change frequently, and the bot's necessary versatility isn't always built-in. Furthermore, a new regulation requiring minor changes to an application form could derail months of back-office work on a bot that is nearly finished.

A new report by Deloitte UK came to the same conclusion. According to Deloitte UK writers Justin Watson, David Wright, and Marina Gordeeva, "only 3% of organisations have managed to scale RPA to a level of 50 or more robots."

Furthermore, the financial benefits of RPA implementations are far from certain. Although it may be possible to automate 30% of activities in the majority of jobs, Edlich and Sohoni argue that this does not always equate to a 30% cost reduction.

See "8 keys to a good RPA implementation" for more information about how to make the transition to RPA go smoothly.

What businesses are using RPA?

Among the many companies using RPA are Walmart, Deutsche Bank, AT&T, Vanguard, Ernst & Young, Walgreens, Anthem, and American Express Global Business Travel.

According to Walmart CIO Clay Johnson, the retail giant has introduced around 500 bots to automate anything from answering employee questions to extracting valuable data from audit records. "A lot of them were from people who were sick of working," Johnson says.

RPA is used by David Thompson, CIO of American Express Global Business Travel, to simplify the process of cancelling and refunding airline tickets. Thompson also wants to use RPA to automate some cost control functions and to facilitate automated rebooking suggestions in the event of an airport closure.

"We've taken RPA and educated it on how workers perform those duties," says Thompson, who previously served as CIO at Western Union and introduced a similar approach. "The list of things we should automate just keeps growing." With more CIOs considering RPA, CIO.com sought advice from some experts about how IT leaders should approach the technology.

10 tips for automating robotic processes effectively:

1. Control and set goals: Fast wins are possible with RPA, but scaling RPA is a different storey. Many RPA issues, according to Dave Kuder, a principal at Deloitte Consulting LLP, stem from a lack of expectations management. Vendors' and implementation consultants' bold statements about RPA haven't helped. That's why CIOs must approach the situation with caution and optimism. "You'll be a lot happier with the outcome if you go in with open eyes," Kuder says.

2. Take into account the financial implications: RPA is often promoted as a way to increase return on investment or cut costs. However, NTT Data Services CTO Kris Fitzgerald believes that more CIOs can use it to enhance customer experience. Airlines, for example, hire thousands of customer service agents, but consumers also have to wait in

line to have their calls answered. A chatbot may be able to help with some of the waiting. "When you put your virtual agent in there, there is no downtime, no sick days, and no negative attitude," Fitzgerald explains. "The customer experience is the red flag to look for."

3. Early and sometimes include IT: When COOs first purchased RPA, they ran into a roadblock during implementation, leading them to seek IT's assistance (and forgiveness), according to Viadro. According to Kuder, "citizen entrepreneurs" with no technical background are now using cloud technologies to incorporate RPA in their business units. Frequently, the CIO will intervene and block them. According to Kuder and Viadro, business leaders must involve IT from the start to ensure that they get the support they need.

4. Change management and poor design can cause havoc: According to Sanjay Srivastava, Genpact's chief digital officer, many implementations fail due to poor design and change management. Some businesses neglect contact exchanges between bots in the rush to get something deployed, which can break a business process. "Think about the operating model architecture before you implement," Srivastava says. "You need to plan out how you want the different bots to interact." Some CIOs, on the other hand, can fail to negotiate the impact of new activities on an organization's business processes. To prevent

business interruption, CIOs must prepare ahead of time.

5. Don't get down into a data rabbit hole: A bank that uses thousands of bots to automate manual data entry or track software operations generates a significant amount of data. This can lead CIOs and their business counterparts into a bad situation where they are attempting to exploit data. According to Srivastava, it's not unusual for companies to run machine learning on the data their bots produce, then add a chatbot to the front to enable users to query the data more easily. Suddenly, the RPA project has morphed into a machine learning project that hasn't been properly scoped. "The puck keeps going," Srivastava says, and CIOs are struggling to keep up. He advises CIOs to think of RPA as a long-term strategy rather than a series of initiatives that morph into something unwieldy.

6. Project management is critical: Another issue that arises in RPA, according to Srivastava, is the inability to prepare for such roadblocks. Since no one configured the bots to adapt when an employee at a Genpact client modified the company's password policy, data was lost. CIOs must continuously monitor for chokepoints where their RPA solution can stutter, or at the very least, add a monitoring and warning system to keep an eye on output hiccups. "You can't just set them free and let them run around; command and control are needed," Srivastava explains.

7. Control ensures compliance: Creating even a single bot in an environment, let alone thousands, poses a number of governance challenges. According to Kuder, one Deloitte client spent multiple meetings trying to figure out whether their bot was male or female, a legitimate gender issue that must be balanced against human resources, ethics, and other areas of business enforcement.

8. Create a world-class RPA base: According to Viadro, the most efficient RPA implementations have a centre of excellence staffed by people who are responsible for ensuring the effectiveness of productivity projects within the company. However, not every business has the financial resources to do so. The RPA centre of excellence creates business cases, calculates possible cost savings and returns on investment, and tracks progress toward those objectives. "The community is usually small and nimble, and it scales with the technology staff that is based on the actual automation implementation," says Viadro. "I will urge all IT leaders in various industries to search for opportunities and determine if [RPA] would be transformative for their organisations."

9. Don't forget about the effect on staff: Some companies are so focused on execution that they forget to include HR, which can lead to nightmare scenarios for workers whose everyday processes

and workflows are disrupted. "We lose sight of the fact that people come first," Fitzgerald says.

10. RPA should be used in the creation process: CIOs must automate the entire production lifecycle or risk their bots being killed during a major launch. "It seems to be easy to recall, but people fail to incorporate it into their routine."

In the end, there is no silver bullet for implementing RPA, according to Srivastava, but it does entail an intelligent automation culture that must be part of an enterprise's long-term journey. "To complete business processes faster, with better efficiency, and at scale, automation needs to get to a response — all of the ifs, then, and whats," Srivastava says.

What Is Edge Computing And Why Is It Important

By getting computing closer to the database, edge computing improves Internet devices and web applications. This reduces latency and bandwidth consumption by reducing the need for long-distance communications between the client and server. Edge computing is a networking concept that focuses on getting computing as close as possible to the source of data to reduce latency and bandwidth use. In layman's terms, edge computing entails transferring fewer processes from the cloud to local locations, such as a user's computer, an IoT system, or an edge server. By bringing computation to the network's edge, the amount of long-distance contact between a client and server is reduced.

What does it mean to be at the network's edge?

The network edge, in the case of Internet devices, is the point at which the computer, or the local network comprising the device, interacts with the Internet. The term "edge" is somewhat ambiguous; for example, a user's device or the processor within an IoT camera may be called the network edge, but so can the user's router, ISP, or local edge server. The key takeaway is that, unlike origin servers and cloud servers, which can be located far away from the devices they connect with, the network edge is physically near to the user.

What sets edge computing apart from other types of computing?

The first computers were huge, bulky devices that could only be reached directly or via terminals that were essentially device extensions. Computing could become even more dispersed thanks to the advent of personal computers. Personal computing was once the most common computing paradigm. Applications ran and data was stored locally on a user's computer, or in an on-premise data centre in some cases. Cloud computing, which is a more recent trend, has a range of advantages over on-premise computing. Cloud services are clustered in a vendor-managed "cloud" (or collection of data centres) and accessible through the Internet from any computer. However, because of the distance between users and the data centres where cloud services are stored, cloud computing can cause latency. Although maintaining the centralised essence of cloud computing, edge computing brings computing closer to end-users to reduce the distance that data must travel.

To sum it up:

Early computing: centralised programmes that were only run on a single computer.

Computers for personal use: Locally managed decentralised applications

Cloud computing refers to the hosting of centralised databases in data centres.

Edge computing refers to centralised systems that run near users, either on the computer or at the network's edge.

What does edge computing entail?

Consider a structure that is protected by a slew of high-definition IoT video cameras. These are "dumb" cameras that simply output a raw video signal and stream it to a cloud server in real-time. The video output from all of the cameras is run via a motion-detection programme on the cloud server, ensuring that only clips of movement are saved to the server's database. This puts a persistent and substantial strain on the building's Internet infrastructure, as the high volume of video footage being transmitted consumes a significant amount of bandwidth. In addition, the cloud server is under a lot of stress because it has to process video from all of the cameras at the same time. Consider moving the motion sensor computation to the network edge. What if each camera ran the motion-detecting application on its own internal computer and then sent the footage to the cloud server as needed? Since much of the camera footage would never have to travel to the cloud server, this would result in a major reduction in bandwidth use. Furthermore, the cloud server will only be responsible for storing the essential video, allowing it to interact with a larger number of cameras without being overburdened. This is how edge computing appears.

What are some other applications for edge computing?

Edge computing can be used in a wide range of products, utilities, and applications. Among the possibilities are:

As previously mentioned, security device monitoring is performed.

IoT devices: For more efficient user experiences, smart devices that connect to the Internet will benefit from running code on the device itself rather than in the cloud.

Self-driving cars: Self-driving cars must respond in real-time, rather than waiting for commands from a server.

Caching that is more efficient: An application can configure how content is cached to more effectively deliver content to users by running code on a CDN edge network.

Medical monitoring devices must respond in real-time without having to wait for a response from a cloud server.

Video conferencing: Because interactive live video consumes a significant amount of bandwidth, bringing backend processes closer to the video source will reduce lag and latency.

What are some of the advantages of edge computing?

1. Cost-cutting: Edge computing, as seen in the example above, helps to reduce bandwidth use and server resources. Bandwidth and cloud resources are restricted, and they are both expensive. Statista estimates that by 2025, there will be over 75 billion IoT devices deployed worldwide, with smart cameras, printers, thermostats, and even toasters in every home and office. Huge quantities of computing would have to be pushed to the edge in order to accommodate both of those devices.

2. Exercising: Reduced latency is another important advantage of shifting processes to the edge. Any

time a computer has to connect with a remote server, a delay is introduced. Two colleagues in the same office speaking over an IM network, for example, can encounter a significant delay since each message must be routed out of the building, communicate with a server somewhere around the globe, and then be brought back until it appears on the recipient's screen. The visible delay would be eliminated if that procedure was moved to the edge and the company's internal router was in charge of transmitting intra-office chats. Users of all types of web applications will experience delays when they encounter processes that require communication with an external server. The length of these delays can differ depending on the server's available bandwidth and location, but they can be avoided entirely by moving more processes to the network edge.

3. New features and functions: Additionally, edge computing can provide previously unavailable features. Edge computing, for example, can be used to process and analyse data at the edge, allowing for real-time processing and analysis.

To summarise, the following are the key advantages of edge computing:

1. Reduced latency

2. Reduced bandwidth consumption and related costs

3. Reduced server capacity and related costs

4. Functionality enhancements

What are some of the disadvantages of edge computing?

Edge computing has the disadvantage of increasing attack vectors. There are new ways for malicious attackers to hack these devices as more "smart" devices, such as edge servers and IoT devices with powerful built-in computers, are added to the mix. Another disadvantage of edge computing is that it necessitates the use of more local hardware. For example, although an IoT camera requires a built-in computer to send raw video data to a web server, running its own motion-detection algorithms would necessitate a much more sophisticated computer with more computing power. However, as hardware costs fall, it becomes more affordable to create smarter devices. Using edge servers is one way to fully eliminate the need for additional hardware.

What is Human Intelligence

Human intelligence is a mental attribute that includes the capacity to learn from experience, adapt to new conditions, comprehend and handle abstract concepts, and manipulate one's surroundings using knowledge. Much of the fascination among intelligence investigators stems from their attempts to define just what intelligence is. In various definitions, different scientists have stressed different characteristics of intelligence. In a 1921 symposium, for example, American psychologists Lewis Terman and Edward L. Thorndike disagreed on how to define intelligence, with Terman emphasising abstract thinking and Thorndike emphasising learning and the capacity to give good answers to questions. However, psychologists have increasingly acknowledged that comprehending both what intelligence is and what it does requires adaptation to the environment. An artist reworks a painting to convey a more coherent impression; a student in school learns the material he needs to know in order to do well in a course; a physician treating a patient with unfamiliar symptoms learns about the underlying disease, or a student in school learns the material he needs to know in order to do well in a course. The adaptation usually entails altering oneself in order to cope better with the environment, but it can also entail changing the environment or finding a whole new one.

Perception, learning, memory, reasoning, and problem-solving are all cognitive functions that are used in effective adaptation. The fundamental emphasis in a definition of intelligence, then, is that it is a selective mixture of cognitive and mental processes that is purposefully directed toward effective adaptation, rather than a single cognitive or mental function. As a result, a physician learning about a new disease adapts by perceiving disease-related material in medical literature, learning what it contains, remembering the critical aspects needed to treat the patient, and then using reason to solve the problem of applying the information to the patient's needs. Intelligence has evolved to be viewed as a collection of skills rather than a single aptitude. However, this has not always been evident to researchers; rather, much of the history of the field revolves around debates over the nature and abilities that make intelligence.

Intelligence theories

Intelligence theories, like other scientific beliefs, have evolved over time through a series of models. Psychometrics, also known as psychometrics, cognitive psychology, which studies the processes by which the mind functions, cognitivism and contextualism, a combined approach that studies the interaction between the environment and mental processes, and biological science, which studies the neural bases of intelligence, are four of the most influential paradigms. The discussion that follows will focus on advances in these four areas.

Theories of psychometrics

Psychometric theories have long sought to comprehend the structure of intelligence: what shape does it take, and what, if any, parts does it contain? Such theories have typically been based on and established by data obtained from mental ability tests, such as analogies (e.g., a lawyer is to a client as a doctor is to __), classifications (e.g., Which word does not belong with the others?), and classifications (e.g., Which word does not belong with the others? robin, sparrow, chicken, blue jay), and series completions (for example, what number follows next in the following series?). (3), (6), (9), (12), (15), (18), (21).....so on

A model underpins psychometric theories in which intelligence is viewed as a collection of talents measured by mental tests. This model is quantifiable. For example, a weighted composite of numerical, reasoning, and memory abilities for a complex series could be represented on a number-series test. Mathematical models allow for a deficiency in one area of test performance to be compensated for by great skill in another. In this sense, strong reasoning skills can compensate for a lack of numerical ability.

The British psychologist Charles E. Spearman (1863–1945), who published his first significant study on intelligence in 1904, is credited with developing one of the earliest psychometric theories. He found something that may seem self-evident now: people who did well on one mental-ability test tended to do well on others, whereas people who did poorly on one tended to do poorly on others. Spearman invented factor analysis, a statistical approach that investigates patterns of individual differences in test scores, to find the underlying reasons of these performance discrepancies. He came to the conclusion that all individual variances in test scores are due to only two types of causes. The first and most essential factor, which he dubbed the "general factor," or g, is present in all intelligence-related tasks. In other words, if a task necessitates intelligence, it necessitates g. The second consideration is unique to each test. When someone takes an arithmetical reasoning test, for example, he must consider a general factor that applies to all exams (g) as well as a specific factor that is tied to whatever mental operations are required for mathematical reasoning as opposed to other types of thinking. But what does g stand for, exactly? After all, naming something does not imply that you know what it is. Spearman didn't know what the general factor was, but in 1927 he speculated that it could be something like "mental energy."

L.L. Thurstone, an American psychologist, disagreed with Spearman's theory, claiming that there were seven elements, which he called "basic mental talents." According to Thurstone, these seven abilities were verbal comprehension (as in vocabulary knowledge and reading), verbal fluency (as in writing and producing words), number (as in solving relatively simple numerical computation and arithmetical reasoning problems), and spatial visualisation (as involved in visualising and manipulating objects, such as fitting a set of suitcases into an automobile trunk), Memory (as in memorising people's names or looks), inductive reasoning (as in completing a number series or forecasting the future based on past experience), and perceptual speed (as involved in rapid proofreading to discover typographical errors in a text). Other psychologists, such as Canadian Philip E. Vernon and American Raymond B. Cattell, have suggested that both Spearman and Thurstone were correct in some ways. Intellectual capacities were considered as hierarchical by Vernon and Cattell, with g, or general ability, at the top of the hierarchy. Below g, however, are tiers of abilities that steadily narrow, culminating in the precise abilities described by Spearman. In Abilities: Their Structure, Growth, and Action (1971), Cattell proposed that general ability can be separated into two types: "fluid" and "crystallised."

Analogies, classifications, and series completions are examples of examinations that assess thinking and problem-solving ability. Vocabulary, general knowledge, and understanding of specific disciplines are examples of crystallised talents, which are assumed to derive from fluid abilities. Crystallized abilities, according to American psychologist John L. Horn, increase more or less across a person's lifetime, whereas fluid abilities increase in early years and decrease in later years. The majority of psychologists believed that Spearman's classification of talents was too limited, but not everyone thought that it should be hierarchical. Joy Paul Guilford, an American psychologist, created a structure-of-intellect hypothesis, which in its earlier iterations proposed 120 talents. Guilford claimed in The Nature of Human Intelligence (1967) that abilities can be classified into five types of operation, four types of content, and six types of product. These characteristics can be mixed and matched to create 120 different abilities. Cognition (operation) of semantic (content) relations (product) is an example of such an ability, which is required in understanding the relationship between lawyer and client in the analogy issue above (the lawyer is to the client as a doctor is to). Guilford eventually extended his theory's proposed number of skills to 150.

It was eventually discovered that the basic approach to psychometric theory has severe flaws. One of the primary manifestations of a movement that began with the postulation of one important skill was the recognition of 150. Furthermore, the psychometricians (as proponents of factor analysis were known) lacked a scientific method for settling their disagreements. Any approach that could support so many possibilities appeared dubious. The psychometric theories, though, failed to reveal anything fundamental about the mechanisms that underpin intelligence. It's one thing to talk about "generic ability" or "fluid ability," but it's quite another to explain what goes on in people's heads when they use the talent in question. Cognitive psychologists argued that the solution to these problems is to research directly the mental processes underlying intelligence and, possibly, to relate them to the dimensions of intelligence provided by psychometricians.

In Human Cognitive Abilities (1993), American psychologist John B. Carroll suggested a "three-stratum" psychometric model of intelligence that built on existing theories of intelligence. Because it is based on reanalyses of hundreds of data sets, many psychologists see Carroll's model as definitive. Carroll recognised restricted abilities (about 50 in number) in the first stratum, which included Thurstone's seven primary abilities. The intermediate layer, according to Carroll, included broad abilities (about 10) such as learning, retrieval ability, speediness, visual perception, fluid intelligence, and idea generation. The general factor, g, was the only factor in the third stratum, as determined by Spearman. Although it may appear self-evident that the top factor is the general factor, this is not the case, because there is no guarantee that there is any general factor at all.

Traditional and current psychometric theories both have their flaws. To begin with, there is no proof that a really general capacity that encompasses all mental talents exists. Contributors to the edited volume The General Factor of Intelligence: How General Is It? (2002), edited by psychologists Robert Sternberg (author of this article) and Elena Grigorenko, offered opposing perspectives on the g factor, with many arguing that specialised abilities are more important than a general ability, especially because they more easily explain why people have different levels of intelligence.

Second, there are psychometric hypotheses that can't accurately describe all that happens in the mind. Third, it's unclear if the tests that underpin psychometric theories are equally applicable across cultures. In fact, it is assumed that success on intelligence or cognitive ability tests will be contingent on one's acquaintance with the cultural context of the people who created the exam. Patricia M. Greenfield, an American psychologist, found in her 1997 study "You Can't Take It with You: Why Ability Assessments Don't Cross Cultures" that a single test can evaluate different talents in different cultures. Her findings highlighted the significance of considering cultural generality while developing ability testing.

Who will win the race Humans or Artificial Intelligence

Human Intelligence is a gift from God to humanity, whereas Artificial Intelligence is a creation of humans. Intelligence, whether human or artificial, plays a critical role. Human intelligence is a trait that aids humans in learning, comprehending, and solving issues with great ideas, whereas artificial intelligence is a system that mimics human intellect based on the data it receives.

You can imagine how much easier our lives would be if machines could do tasks identical to those performed by the human brain. Are you still debating whether or not artificial intelligence can match human intelligence?

Let's get right to the point and learn the difference between artificial intelligence and human intelligence. This book also discusses the role of artificial intelligence in the human world, artificial intelligence vs. human intelligence, artificial intelligence's effects on the future of jobs and the economy, and many other topics in depth.

AI is rapidly advancing, helping humans to become more productive and live a more balanced life.

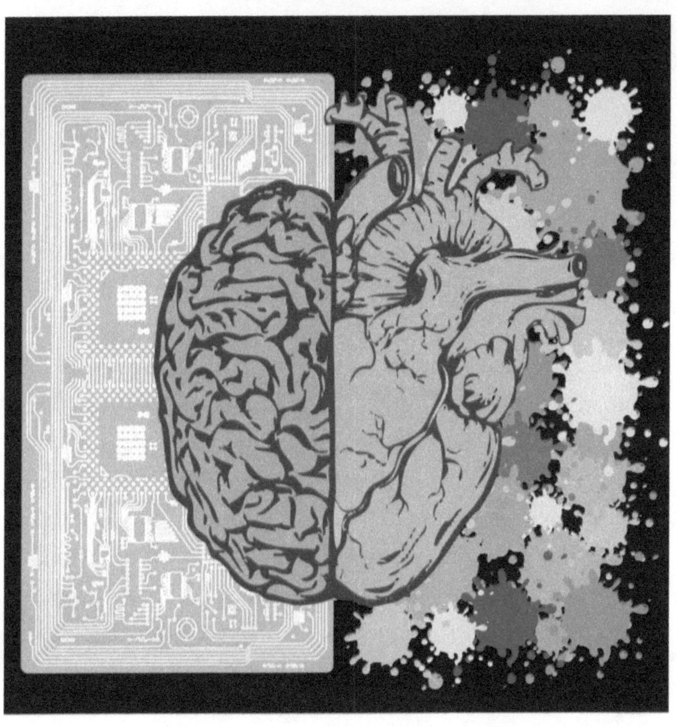

Human intelligence refers to a person's academic ability to think, learn from various expressions, absorb complicated ideas, solve numerical problems, adapt to new situations, influence one's surroundings, and communicate with other people. What makes human intellect so astonishing is that it is fueled by abstract emotions like enthusiasm and inspiration, which enable humans to complete difficult psychological tasks.

In the human world, what role does artificial intelligence play?

Numerical cycles affect increasing calculating capability to deliver faster and more exact models and estimates of operational systems, or improved depictions and blends of large data sets, which are the foundations of artificial intelligence improvements. Nonetheless, while these ground-breaking inventions can do specific tasks with greater efficiency and precision, human skill plays a critical role in designing and implementing AI innovation. Human intelligence is what shapes the growth and appropriation of man-made awareness, as well as the creative arrangements that go with it. Through simple reasoning, human intellect seeks to answer the question "why" and considers "imagine a scenario where." Because complicated issues and the nature of information continue to put engineering design to the test, human oversight, competence, and quality assurance are essential when using AI-generated results.

Human Intelligence v/s Artificial Intelligence

The concept of creating a machine that can think like a human has made its way from science fiction to reality. Robots can perform tasks that were previously impossible. We've been trying for a long time to get Artificial Intelligence in Machines to help us with our work.

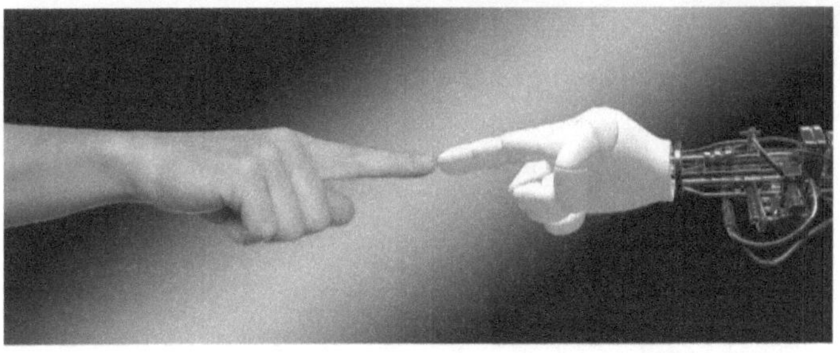

From a variety of perspectives, there are bots, humanoids, robots, and programmed humans who either outflank people or organise with us. When compared to people, these AI-driven apps execute faster, have more operational capacity, and are more precise, while also being profoundly large in dismal and monotonous roles.

Human intelligence, on the other hand, is associated with a wide range of knowledge and experience. It doesn't usually rely on pre-processed data like the ones required for AI. When compared to the machine's equipment and programming foundation, human memory, its recording capability, and the human body as an element may appear to be insignificant. However, our brain's depth and layers are far more unexpected and complicated, and machines will never be able to match them, at least not anytime soon.

The major differences between artificial intelligence and human intelligence are as follows:

- If we compare it to nature, human intelligence aims to adapt to current circumstances by combining a variety of cognitive functions, whereas artificial intelligence aims to construct gadgets that mimic human behaviour and do human-like behaviours. As a result, the human brain is analogue, whereas computers are digital.

- The simple distinction is that humans employ their brains, thinking abilities, and memory, whereas AI computers rely on data provided to them.

- Humans, as we all know, learn from their mistakes, and clever ideas and attitudes are the foundation of human intellect. As a result, this claim is simply made since machines are incapable of thinking and learning from the past. They can learn through information and frequent training, but they will never be able to think in the way that people do.

- Artificial intelligence (AI) is a type of machine learning that a long time to respond to new changes, whereas humans adapt quickly to new situations, allowing them to learn and master a variety of skills.

- Modern computers typically consume 2 watts of power, whereas the human brain consumes approximately 25 watts.

- When compared to people, machines can handle more data at a faster rate. Humans cannot currently match the speed of computers.

- Artificial Intelligence (AI) has yet to master the ability to pick up on connected social and exciting codes. People are better at social connection in many aspects because they can develop academic data, have self-awareness, and are sensitive to the feelings of others.

What influence will AI have on jobs and the economy in the future?

- **Tasks can be automated:**The most visible impact of AI is the result of task automation across a wide range of industries, which has shifted from manual to digital. Tasks or professions that need a high level of repetition or the use and translation of massive amounts of data are now delivered and handled by computers, often without the need for human intervention.

- **New opportunities are always welcome:**Artificial intelligence and machine learning automate tasks that formerly required human intervention, allowing new firms to emerge and opportunities to open for the labour force. Digital engineering is an example of a new profession that arose as a result of rapid technological advancements, and it is still evolving. As a result, while old manual jobs may be phased out, new opportunities and professions will emerge.

- **Model of economic development:** Artificial intelligence, when employed for a purpose rather than for the sake of technology, can open up a plethora of opportunities for businesses and improve efficiency and collaboration inside the organisation. As a result, it can lead to an increase in demand for goods and services, as well as a monetary development model that conveys and improves the quality of life.

- **Workplace responsibilities:** Understanding the capacity of employment beyond simply maintaining a way of life is far more important in the age of AI. It gives the appearance of a critical human need for investment, co-creation, commitment, and a sense of being needed, and so should not be overlooked. So, every now and again, even the most mundane and uninteresting tasks at work become significant and valuable, and if they are eliminated or robotized, they should be replaced with something that provides a similar opportunity for human expression and revelation.

- **New world for for invention and creativity:**With the rise of robotics, artificial intelligence, and robotization, some of the mundane and manual duties off our plates, experts will have more time to focus on reasoning, transmitting new and ingenious arrangements, and other activities that are beyond the scope of AI and squarely within the realm of human intellect.

To summarise, artificial intelligence has progressed from a science fiction concept to a reality, and there is no doubt that it is transforming every industry and propelling the globe forward.

However, it is still impossible to exactly duplicate human intelligence. Experts believe that computers will not be able to duplicate human thought processes in the near future. Because scientists and experimenters are still baffled by the maze that lies beneath the human brain process. It's exceedingly unlikely that we'll ever create machines that can think like humans.

"Full artificial intelligence development could herald the end of humanity.... It would take off on its own, re-designing itself at an ever-faster pace. Humans, whose biological evolution is slowed, would be unable to compete and would be surpassed." - According to Professor Stephen Hawking.

As a result, in the ongoing debate over artificial intelligence vs. human intellect, the general consensus has been that artificial intelligence will augment rather than replace human tasks in the near future.

Why do I call them the "Army of Metalloids"

As we studied in Chapter 3rd "What is Metalloid?" exactly Metalloids are semiconductors. Integrated circuits are the foundation of practically all modern technology. It's a small square or rectangle of semiconductor material, usually silicon, that holds electronic circuits that are laid down or grown to perform computation or other functions. The idea was to embed a large number of transistors and other devices onto a single piece of silicon and construct the interconnections within the silicon. Electronic components such as transistors, resistors, diodes, inductors, and capacitors were manually connected together on a board before the integrated circuit. By combining components into a single chip of material, the integrated circuit enabled more powerful, lightweight, and smaller applications.

Texas Instruments' Jack Kilby got the US patent #3,138,743 for miniaturised electronic circuits, while Fairchild Semiconductor's Robert Noyce received the US patent #2,981,877 for a silicon-based integrated circuit in 1959. After years of legal wrangling (until 1966), the two businesses decided to cross-license each other's patents, resulting in the birth of the IC industry.

Analog, digital, and mixed-signal circuits are the three basic types of integrated circuits. Integrated circuits can be monolithic — consisting of a single piece of silicon with components placed in one layer — or more complex, such as chiplets with many pieces of silicon. Transistors, contacts, and interconnects make up a digital integrated circuit. However, there is an inflection moment in the development of leading-edge processors. The transistor acts as a switch and is located at the bottom of the structure. The interconnects, which are located on top of the transistor, are made up of small copper wiring schemes that transport electrical impulses from one transistor to the next. A layer termed the middle-of-line joins the transistor structure and interconnects (MOL). A succession of small contact structures makes up the MOL layer.

The two primary design steps are handled differently by the IC design flows for digital, analogue, and mixed-signal chips:

design and testing of functional elements

verification of the physical design

The transistors are made at the front-end-of-the-line (FEOL), contacts are made at the middle-of-the-line (MOL), and interconnects are made at the backend-of-the-line (BEOL) in the IC manufacturing process. The process then moves on to testing and packaging.

Artificial Intelligence Is A Lot More Than You Might Think

We've got our fill of discussing What Is Artificial Intelligence? What examples can you give, and how does it work? Similarly, we will go over this in greater detail in our book.

Artificial Intelligence is based on the use of clever and advancing algorithms to combine massive amounts of data. Algorithms currently play the job of allowing software (machines) to extract knowledge from the data's insights, information, and patterns.

Not only that, but AI on a bigger scale encompasses a variety of additional elements such as technology, processes, and theories. Machine Learning, Deep Learning, Neural Networks, Evolutionary Computation Vision, Robotics, Expert Systems, Speech Processing, Cognitive Computing, Natural Language Processing, and other AI technologies are required to perform well.

Artificial Intelligence's Major Subsets:

- **Artificial Intelligence:**It is a major component of AI, and its purpose is to strengthen AI and propel it forward to new heights. Machine Learning enables AI to concentrate on building the ability to enhance reactions and outputs in each given situation based on previous data experiences. Deep learning is a subset of machine learning that helps AI solve and understand multidimensional complicated patterns and data sets and draws solutions from them. Rule-based machine learning, on the other hand, has given AI a new dimension, as it is built on a conceptual set of rules. It refers to a set of techniques that allow a machine to identify rules without the need for human intervention, rather than relying on manually curated rules as in standard rule-based ML.

- **Speech Recognition:** Here, AI is trained/programmed to detect words, sayings, or phrases in a given language, translate them into machine-understandable codes, then reverse or respond to them. AI can now turn audio communications into text or vice versa and can detect human voices such as SIRI, Alexa, or OK Google, thanks to the improvement in speech processing.

- **Network of Neurons:** The goal of AI is to emulate human behaviour, whether it's communication, vision, or intelligence. Human brains activate neural network algorithms, and the way they work aids in data collection, recognition, connection, and problem-solving. The major goal of this subgroup is to work in the same way that a human would.

- **Processing of Natural Language:** Natural Language Processing, as the name suggests, is a subset of AI that is capable of understanding human-generated language, including speech. In certain ways, NPL gets meaning from human contact in order to complete its job. Developers only need to format the data before instructing the computer to perform tasks like automatic summarization, translation, named entity recognition, relationship extraction, sentiment analysis, audio recognition, and topic segmentation.

These technologies are implemented in semiconductor integrated circuits like the soul into the body. In other words, examples of the pen body and its refill. Here pen body is semiconductor integrated circuits and the refill is artificial intelligence technologies. If the statement given by Professor Stephen Hawking, other researchers and scientist comes true, then it will chaos for the entire mankind. Humanity has to face the Army of Metalloids.

Conclusion

- Popular AI fantasies include an island populated by mechanical devices and self-driving autos. This approach, however, fails to recognise that AI's critical function is in the practical application, processing, and management of massive volumes of data generated on a regular basis. Other key applications of AI include acquiring information and automating processes. AI works on wise searches, deciphering all types of files, be it text, audio, or image, to uncover the pattern and then act accordingly, based on the bulk data provided by people.

- **The text must have taught you what it is to be human and how it relates to intelligence.**

- Artificial intelligence is now being used in the business world. If AI could achieve the same degree of intelligence as a human. It's also possible that it'll take control of the entire global economy.

- The book must have given you an understanding of what AI is and how it is applied to a computer in doing various jobs; every portion of it requires an algorithm to function.

- **If Professor Stephen Hawking's and other academics' and scientists' predictions come true, the world will be in pandemonium. The Army of Metalloids must be faced by humanity.**

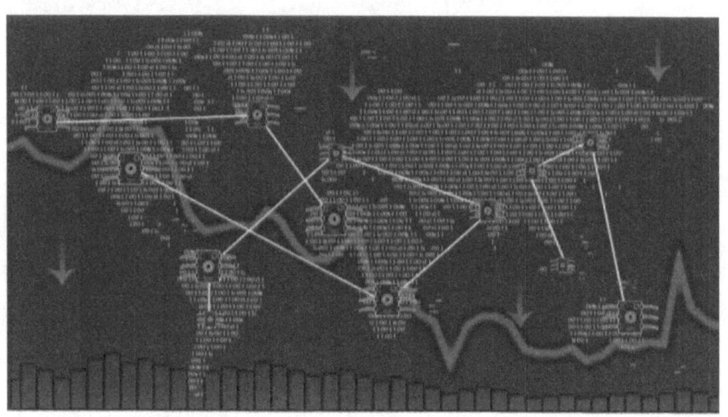